Owen Ruffhead

Reasons why the approaching treaty of peace should be debated in Parliament

Owen Ruffhead

Reasons why the approaching treaty of peace should be debated in Parliament

ISBN/EAN: 9783337224820

Printed in Europe, USA, Canada, Australia, Japan

Cover: Foto ©Suzi / pixelio.de

More available books at **www.hansebooks.com**

REASONS

WHY THE

Approaching TREATY of PEACE

SHOULD BE

Debated in PARLIAMENT:

As a Method most Expedient and Constitutional.

In a LETTER addressed to a GREAT MAN.

AND

Occasioned by the Perusal of a Letter addressed to
TWO GREAT MEN.

---

*Lex justissima, provida circumspectione stabilita, ut quod omnes
tangit, ab omnibus approbetur.* Clause of a Writ of Edw. I.

LONDON:

Printed for R. GRIFFITHS, opposite Somerset-
house, in the Strand.
MDCCLX.

R E A S O N S, &c.

S I R,

THE truly patriot Spirit which you have fhewn during the Continuance of your fhort but glorious Adminiftration, the Attention you have paid to every Hint for the public Good, without regarding from what Quarter it proceeded, naturally encourages every Well-wifher to to his Country to offer his Sentiments on the Profpect of an approaching Peace.

Pardon me, Sir, the Prefumption of adding one to the numerous Addreffes which have been made to you on this Occafion. As I am perfuaded that *they* are moft patient of Remonftrance who are beft able to give Advice, I flatter myfelf that the Liberty will not offend you.

I do not pretend, Sir, to adminifter Council, but only to ftate Matter for your, and the public, Confideration. If what I pro-

B   pofe

pose is worthy of Attention, it will reach your Notice; if not, it will deservedly perish with those many fugitive Productions, which breathe their last before they are well delivered from the Press.

My Proposal, such as it is, was suggested by the Perusal of a Pamphlet, entitled, *A Letter addressed to Two Great Men*, wherein a Passage occurred, which induced me to deliver my Thoughts on the Subject of that Treatise.

Perhaps it would not be difficult for me to point out the Letter-writer by Name; but as his Sentiments only are the proper Objects of public Consideration, an Attempt to discover his Person, might be justly deemed idle and impertinent.

Whoever he is, he appears to be well experienced in national Affairs, and not unaccustomed to handle his Pen. We may, in many Parts, perceive Flashes of that Spirit, which so greatly contributed to drive a late powerful Minister from the Helm of State, which he had so long directed against all the Torrent of Opposition: And from some distant Allusions to the turbulent Transactions of those Times, we may discover the Letter-writer to be a Veteran in Politicks.

With

With regard to the Terms which he thinks neceffary to be infifted upon at the Conclufion of a Peace, he may, in fome Inftances, perhaps, be deemed too fanguine. But if, on particular points, he difcovers an Exuberance of Zeal, yet, upon the Whole, in my humble Apprehenfion, he appears to be intelligent and difcreet.

But I do not mean to enter into any Difquifition relating to the Particulars of his Propofals. None, *confidered as Individuals*, are better capable of judging what are the proper Terms of Peace, than they who have conducted the War to fuch a happy and glorious Iffue. But a Point of fuch Importance feems to merit the confideration of a collective Body.

Therefore, leaving the Terms of the expected Treaty to wifer Confideration, I beg Leave to offer fome few Obfervations with refpect to the *Method of negociating*.

The Terms to be obtained by the enfuing Negociation will, I apprehend, in a great Meafure depend on the Method of treating. This is the primary Object of Attention, and cannot be too minutely confidered.

Whatever is conducive to a profitable and glorious Accommodaion, is of the utmoft Importance to this Kingdom. A good and

ftable

ſtable Peace alone can enſure the Proſperity, nay, the very Being of this Nation.

However we may flatter ourſelves in the ſmiling Hours of Triumph, that we are ſound and vigorous, yet it will require many Years of uninterrupted Peace, to recover from the Diſorders and Calamities of War.

It will be our own Faults, if we do not ſecure a full Opportunity of ſtrengthening and ſecuring our Conſtitution. Tho' our Strength is debilitated, that of the Enemy is utterly exhauſted. We may preſcribe our own Terms, and compell them to accept of our Propoſals.

To give away with the Pen, as we have done formerly, the Advantages gained by the Sword, would be an Inſtance of moſt unpardonable Inattention. The Enemy has no Reſource but in Perfidy and Chicane : We know their Diſpoſition, and ought not to leave them an Opportunity of fruſtrating their Engagements by the Arts of Quibble and Intrigue.

It may be imprudent, therefore, to hazard a diſtant Negociation. The Letter-writer propoſes to fix the Scene at Home, and to name no other Plenipotentiaries to conduct the Peace, but thoſe Miniſters who directed the War.

This Propoſal is wiſe and juſt. To ſee the Direction of the Treaty in ſuch Hands, would

would give univerfal Satisfaction, and afford
the ftrongeft Affurance of its being concluded with Skill and Integrity. But I beg
Leave to extend the Propofition.

The Letter-writer, Sir, premifes, that
" by the Extinction of factious Oppofition,
the Channel of parliamentary Inftruction is
ftopped, fo that no other but that of the
Prefs is left open, for thofe Heads of Advice
to which it may be worth a Minifter's while
to attend."

This is the Paffage, Sir, which ftruck me
with Concern, and opened a Train of
Thought, which gave Birth to the Propofition
which I fhall recommend in the Sequel.

Surely it muft furprize, and grieve every
Lover of the *Britifh* Conftitution to hear,
from fuch good Authority, that the Extinction of factious Oppofition by the happy
Unanimity of every Party, fhould have clofed
the Channel of parliamentary Inftruction.
Can Inftruction then never reach the Ears of
a Minifter in Parliament, but from the
Mouth of Oppofition ?

I ufe the Word Oppofition here, in the Senfe
in which the Letter-writer employs it; not
as denoting a Difference of Opinion, but a
Variance of Party, and Difagreement of
Faction.

Inftruction

Inftruction conveyed through fuch a Channel, can ferve only to gratify Malignity on
one Hand, and mortify Pride on the other.
It is like the Application of a Cauftick,
which muft torture the Patient, before it can
operate to his Benefit.

No one, Sir, can entertain a higher Notion
of the Dignity of Parliaments than myfelf, or
bear greater Refpect to their Authority. For
the Honour, therefore, of thofe auguft Af-
femblies, nay, for the Credit of human Nature, I am unwilling to believe, that nothing
but Enmity to a Minifter can open the
Mouths of our Reprefentatives, and that fe-
natorial Eloquence has its Root in Faction.

Such a Suppofition, Sir, would be, in the
higheft degree, injurious to the Reputation
of Parliament. Every one is prefumed to
come there with a Difpofition and an Abi-
lity to ferve his Country. Confequently
they will be earneft in communicating whatever they deem effential to that Purpofe, and
refolute in oppofing whatever they apprehend to have a contrary Tendency.

The Difcharge of thefe Duties, fuppofes
them neither biaffed by their Connections
with one Party*, or prejudiced by their Enmity

* I ufe Party here in *pejorem Senfum.* An Affocia-
tion for the Purpofe of refifting Oppreffion or redref-
fing

mity to another. A real Concern for the common Welfare, will direct every Speech, and determine every Vote. They will remember that they are summoned together to council, not to wrangle; to debate, not to dictate.

If the worst of Avarice is that of Sense, the Parcimony is doubly criminal in a Senator. To advise, is the Privilege, nay, the Duty, of every one in Parliament; to direct, can be the Lot but of a few. Men may be unanimous about the End, yet differ with respect to the Means.

But such is the Pride of human Nature, that they who have a Capacity for advising, aspire to govern. Not content to draw in friendly Concert with others of equal Abilities, they are eager to take the Lead, and scorn to assist those whom they cannot rule.

It is difficult to conceive any thing more mortifying and deplorable, than to see Faction, disappointed in its towering Views of Ambition, sit down in sullen Silence, and acquiesce with affected Unanimity.

Unanimity I cannot call it, since the Mind has no share in the Acquiescence. It is at

fing Grievances, is not a Party in the appropriated Sense of the Word. As *Sallust* observes, *Hæc inter Bonos Amicitia, inter Malos Factio est.*

beft

beſt but a negative Union. Neceſſity com-
pells an outward Conformity, but the Will
yet continues in Oppoſition.

An Union of this Kind, is like a broken
Glaſs decorated with curious Painting. The
Colours hide the Flaw, but do not repair
the Fracture.

I am willing to ſuppoſe, however, that
there is a farther, and pardon me if I ſay a
better, Reaſon than that aſſigned by the in-
genious and worthy Letter-writer, why the
Channel of parliamentary Inſtruction is ſtop-
ped on the Subject of the expected Treaty
of Peace.

As the Power of denouncing War, and
concluding Peace, are among the grand Prerogatives of the Crown, it might be inde-
cent, perhaps, in the Parliament to anticipate the royal Deciſion, by recommending
Terms of Accommodation.

Such a Liberty might be thought to en-
trench too far on the Sovereign's Prerogative ; of which every loyal and dutiful Subject will be more than commonly tender.
No Prince ever exerciſed it with ſuch Lenity and Caution, or ever was more ſcrupu-
louſly attentive to the Preſervation of public
Freedom.

To

To open the Channel of Parliamentary Inftruction therefore, without trefpaffing on
the royal Prerogative, or violating the fub-
fifting Unanimity, and thereby eſtabliſh the
moſt efficacious Method of conducting a
Treaty of Peace, is the Defign of the prefent Treatife.

To accompliſh this great and defirable
End, you, Sir, may be the noble Inſtrument.
As the moſt effectual Means to attain it, it
depends upon you, to difpofe our Patriot Sovereign gracioufly to *confult* with his faithful
and affectionate Parliament at this important
Crifis, with regard to the Terms of the enfuing Negociation.

The Parliament is aptly ftiled the King's
Grand Council. Who fo fit, under the Royal
Favour, for debating about the Terms of
Peace, as they who have fo chearfully and
generoufly voted fuch large Supplies for pro-
fecuting the War ?—Supplies, indeed, which
were not granted in vain, fince they have
been moſt profitably and glorioufly applied.

Such a Condefcenfion in the Crown, would
endear his Majefty's Memory to the lateft
Pofterity, and do farther Honour, Sir, to
your Adminiſtration. It would be the
brighteſt Circumftance in the ſhining An-
nals of thefe Times. It would argue that
kind Confidence in the Wifdom and Affec-

C   tion

tion of Parliament, which alone, in a Government conftituted like ours, can make a King happy, and the Nation profperous. A firm Union between the King and People, under a free Conftitution, adds greater Strength and Security to a Kingdom, than all the Fleets and Armies which a Treafury can purchafe.

The Unanimity which now happily fubfifts in Parliament, feems to invite fuch Confidence. The Rectitude of the Meafures which have been purfued; and the unparalelled Succefs with which they have been crowned, has conciliated all difinterefted Minds, and even forced Faction to diffemble Conformity.

Such a Difpofition affords the faireft Opportunity of *reviving a Practice* which is confonant to Reafon, and, as I hope to fhew, agreeable to the Conftitution.

The Letter-writer himfelf obferves, that " the wifeft Meafures have been pointed out in the Courfe of Parliamentary Debate; and that Members of either Houfe, perhaps thofe leaft confulted by Government, have frequently been earlieft in fuggefting fuch Plans of Policy, as Government itfelf has been glad to adopt."

Shall

Shall then the Benefit of fuch public Deliberation be loft, on fo important an Occafion? What Subject more 'interefting can
engage the Attention of Parliament? Shall
the Reprefentatives of the Nation be fummoned together to furnifh the Means of Victory, and fhall not they be confulted about
the Difpofal of the Fruits of Conqueft?

Can any valid Reafon be affigned, why a
Treaty of Peace fhould not be debated as
well as an Act of Parliament? Perhaps all
the Statutes combined, which have paffed
this Seffion, are not of half the Confequence
to the Honour and Intereft of the Kingdom,
as the approaching Treaty.

If the Scene of Negotiation is fixed at
Home, and the Terms of the Treaty deli-
berated upon in Parliament, fuch Regula-
tions will deter the Enemy from offering
trifling and evafive Propofals and Objections.

Should it be fuppofed, however, that fuch
a Method would protract the Negotiation,
by Means of the various and lengthened Debates which may arife on the Subject, it may
be anfwered, that in a Confideration of Peace,
in our Circumftances as Victors, the Delay
cannot be dangerous.

In Matters of War, and other Concerns
which require Vigor and Difpatch, or Se-

crecy,

crecy, it is juft that the Sovereign, with whom the Executive Power is wifely lodged, fhould act of his own mere Motion, or by the Advice of his Privy Council.

Great Bodies are not proper to deliberate about Affairs which require prompt Execution. Before they can come to a Determination, perhaps the critical Moment on which Succefs depends, is irretrievably loft.

But in important Cafes, the Refult of which depend more on mature Confideraticn, than on the Vigour of Execution, great Bodies are undoubtedly moft fitting to hold Confultation.

Where all are interefted, all fhould be confulted; unlefs fome impending Danger renders it hazardous to collect the Advice of many. In the Words of my Motto, *It is a moft juft Law, eftablifhed with the moft provident Circumfpection, that what concerns all fhould be approved by all.*

This is agreeable likewife to the Policy of our *German* Forefathers, as appears from *Tacitus. De minoribus Rebus* PRINCIPES *confultant, De Majoribus* OMNES.

In time of Peace, their Princes were no more than great Judges: As may not only be gathered from the Hiftorian above cited, but from *Cæfar*, who fays, *In Pace nullus*

com-

communis eft magiftratus, fed Principes regio-
num atque pagonum inter fuos jus dicunt, con-
troverfiafque minuunt. What related to national Affairs was debated in the great Affembly.

Perhaps no Subject ever engaged the Attention of Parliament, fince the Revolution,
of more Importance to the Honour and Welfare of this Kingdom, than the approaching
Treaty.

Public Expectation hangs upon it, and an-
ticipates the Glory and Security which is to
arife from it. Every one is fenfible of our
Power to do ourfelves Juftice; every one is
convinced of the Neceffity of exerting that
Power with Refolution and Difcretion.

Under fuch Circumftances, why fhould a
Treaty be concluded in the Dark? Why
fhould not the Parliament be confulted on a
Tranfaction of fuch uncommon Moment?
The extraordinary Zeal and Attachment
which has been defervedly fhewn to his Majefty's Perfon and Government, feems to merit fuch Condefcenfion; and the Unanimity
and Wifdom of Parliament, to deferve fuch
Confidence.

Happily, Sir, we are not now in the Condition we were at the Peace of *Utrecht.* It is
not neceffary for you to intrigue Under-hand
with

with *French* Agents and *French* Spies. Nor would you submit to such base Modes of Negociation.

It is not neceffary for you, to expedite a Peace on any Conditions, in Order to fecure yourfelf and Friends in Power, and defeat the Intereft of an oppofite Party, whofe Influence depends on the Continuance of the War.

Thefe, among others, were the Caufes which produced that difadvantageous and inglorious Treaty. The *French* knew the Perplexity in which the felfifh Views of the Minifters involved the Adminiftration, and they prudently took Advantage of this Embarraffment.

The Cafe now is widely different. The Unanimity which fubfifts among all Orders of Men: The Wifdom, Integrity, and Spirit of the Adminiftration, deprive the Enemy of all Hopes of impofing upon us by difhonourable and delufive Terms.

They know that it is not fo much our Intereft, as theirs, to accelerate a Peace. It is our Bufinefs, they are fenfible, to deliberate maturely on every Article, that the Expofition of the Treaty may not hereafter be left to the Interpretation of Commiffaries. For

once

once we may make the imperious Enemy wait our Leifure.

If the Treaty is debated in Parliament, fuch folemn Deliberation will not only give it additional Weight with our Enemies, but with all other interefted Powers.

Such a confpicuous Proof of firm Confidence between a triumphant King and his victorious People, will caufe all *Europe* to admire, dread, and refpect the *Britifh* Crown and Nation.

It may be objected, perhaps, that in a Debate of this Kind there will be a great Difference of Opinions, and Diverfity of Propofitions, which may tend to perplex the Negociation. But probably fuch Contrariety will rather tend to remove Difficulty, than introduce Perplexity.

Many, no Doubt, of fanguine Expectations, will be eager in infifting upon Terms of Parade and Vain Glory. But cooler Judgments will correct their Impetuofity.

The moft rational Triumph after a Victory, is Moderation. The Infolence of Conqueft debafes the Merit of the Conqueror. It mortifies the Enemy's Pride more than a Defeat, and whets his Appetite for future Revenge.

It

It tends likewife to inflame the Jealoufy and provoke the Animofity of other Powers. Among States, as among Individuals, the Arrogance of Superiority never fails to give Offence and create Enmity.

But a moderate Ufe of fuperior Power, on the other Hand, alleviates the Enemy's Sufferings, foftens his Difgrace, and perhaps may reconcile him to his Fate: While, at the fame time, it removes the envious and jealous Apprehenfions of other States, who may become Friends to the Victor, when they fee him ufe the Prerogatives of Conqueft with fo much Lenity and Juftice.

Our Sovereign has afforded the World a fignal Proof, that he not only knows how to conquer, but how to employ Victory to the noble Purpofes.of Juftice and Humanity. Even in the giddy Hour of Triumph, his royal Breaft fwells with Compaffion, and mourns the Effufion of Chriftian Blood. Forced into a War in his own Defence, victorious in all Parts of the Globe, he forgives his Wrongs, forgets his Conquefts, and gracioufly offers that Peace, which his Enemies dared not afk.

Something however is due to the Honour of the Nation. Reputation, in one Senfe, is Power: And it becomes us at leaft to efface

face thofe Stains, which remain as fo many Reproaches on our Character.

As the Enemy therefore at the Conclufion of the laft Peace, compelled us to the degrading Neceffity of pledging Hoftages of our Faith, it may be advifeable to oblige them to make us Reparation in this Refpect, by fending two Noblemen of equal or fuperior Rank, as Pledges of their faithful Performance of thofe Conditions which may not admit of immediate Execution.

But obftinately to infift on Terms purely of Vain Glory, where the Vindication of our Honour, formerly injured in the fame Inftance, does not juftify our Pertinacity, is highly impolitick and unjuft. Yet many, as I have obferved, of warm Temperature, will be earneft in recommending fuch violent Extremities.

Others, it may eafily be forefeen, fwayed by private Interefts and Attachments, will make their own partial Views the Foundation of their feveral Propofitions and Objections.

Some probably will argue with the Letter-Writer, that the Poffeffion of *Guadaleupe* need not be made a neceffary Condition of the Peace, as we have fo many Sugar-Iflands of our own : And that *Senegal* and *Goree* are not of Confequence enough to make us

D   Amends

Amends for the annual Mortality of our brave Countrymen to guard our African Coasts.

Others, on the contrary, biassed by opposite Interests, or prejudiced by different Propensities, will consider the Retention of those Places as the *sine quibus non* of Accommodation. They may think, with Respect to *Guadaloupe* in particular, that our Sugar Plantations being in too few Hands, the Extension of the Trade by the Possession of *Guadaloupe* would be of general Benefit.

But from this clashing of various particular Interests, and from this Opposition of Sentiment, your Discernment will better enable you to discover the general Interest, and to form your Conclusions accordingly.

You, Sir, will probably have no Objection to the Method which I have the Honour to propose of negociating a Peace in Parliament. You will there have a public Opportunity of displaying your Abilities in Negociation, and of convincing the World that your Skill in managing a Treaty of Peace, is equal to your Spirit in conducting the War.

By the Power of your Eloquence and the Solidity of your Arguments, you will be able to silence inexpedient Propositions, and to remove groundless Objections. You will gain
more

more Honour by fuch public Deliberation, than you can hope to acquire by a Treaty managed in the Cabinet ; where your Country will only fee the Refult of your Judgment, without hearing the Reafons of your Refolutions.

Such a public Mode of Negociation, Sir, will moreover be the Means of preventing all future Murmurings and Difcontent. It will fruftrate the Defigns of factious Enemies at Home, if there are any fuch whom your Virtues have not reconciled, and utterly defeat their Hopes of pretending Imperfections in the Treaty, as the Means to difcredit your Negociation, and to remove you from a Poft where you are fo obnoxious to the Sons of Mammon and Corruption.

Though by Extinction of Oppofition therefore, or through Tendernefs for the Prerogative, the Channel of parliamentary Inftruction be clofed on the Subject of the approaching Negociation, yet, when the Parliament is required by his Majefty to confult on that Head, it will be opened for the moft noble and liberal Purpofes. Every one then may freely declare his Opinion, though, till then, it might not be decent in any one to anticipate what is the proper Object of royal Confideration only.

It may be thought however by fome, that the Method propofed is not ftrictly conftitu-

tional.

tional. To thofe who are but little verfed in Antiquity, the Revival of antient Cuftom may bear the Appearance of modern Innovation.

I therefore beg Leave to enumerate fome Inftances where the Kings of *England* have condefcended to confult with their Parliaments * on the Subjects of Peace and War. Inftances, Sif, which, though familiar to your Recollection, will, I am perfuaded, be new to many of my Readers.

It would be eafy for me to trace this Practice beyond the *Norman* Period, or even beyond the Time of the *Anglo Saxons :* But as fuch an Inveftigation might feem rather calculated for vain Parade than fubftantial Proof, I fhall confine myfelf to fuch Examples as occur fince the Conqueft.

The firft which I fhall produce for this Purpofe is in the Time of King *John.* There is the firft Summons on Record to the Peers or Barons, *Tracturi de Magnis & arduis Nego- tiis.* The Particular Bufinefs was about a War of Defence againft the *French :* And that the Commons were admitted at this Time may be concluded from the following

* I ufe the word *Parliament* here to fignify the great Affembly of the Nation ; as it was formerly called *Commune Confilium* or *Magnum Concilium.* At what Time Parliaments took the prefent Model is ftill a *Texata Quæftio,* and foreign from my Difcuffion.

Ordi-

Ordinance : *Provifum eft affenfu Archiepifco-*
porum, Comitum, Baronum, et OMNIUM FI-
DELIUM NOSTRORUM ANGLIÆ, *quod novem*
milites par Angliam inveniend. decimarum,
&c.

The next is in the 49th of *Henry* the 3d,
when a Parliament was called to *advife* with
the King *pro* PACE *affecuranda & firmanda.*
Thefe are the Words of the Writ ; and,
where Advice is required, Confultation muft
neceffarily be admitted.

His Son, *Edward* the 1ft, who for his
Wifdom was ftiled the *Englifh Juftinian,* upon hearing that the *French* King intended to
invade Part of his Inheritance, fummoned
a Parliament, and in the Writ for that Purpofe inferted thofe admirable Words which
I have chofen for my Motto *.

His Son, *Edward* the 2d, affembled a Parliament to advife *fuper diverfis negotiis ftatum*
regni & expeditionem Guerræ Scctiæ fpecialiter
tangentibus. In the 13th Year of his Reign
a Parliament was called to advife, *fuper ar-*
duis negotiis ftatum Gafconiæ tangentibus: And
in the 16th, to confult *ad refrænandum Scoto-*
rum obftinentiam & militiam.

---

* It is obfervable that the Words of the Motto fpeak
of this Practice as a *Law.* But perhaps this is not a proper Time for infifting on the Revival of fuch a Practice
as a *Right.*

Edward

Edward the 3d, in the firft Year of his Reign, fummoned a Parliament *fuper præmiffis tractare & confilium impendere*, before he would *refolve upon Peace or War* with the *Scotch* King.

In the fifth Year of his Reign, the Chancellor declared to the Parliament the Caufe of their being affembled, which was to confult and refolve, whether the King fhould proceed with *France* for Recovery of his Seignories, by Alliance of Marriage, or by War? And whether he fhould go over in Perfon or not, to fuppreſs the Difobedience of the *Irifh*?

In the 13th Year, the Parliament is reaffembled to advife *de expeditione Guerræ in partibus tranfmarinis*; and Ordinances were made for Provifion of Ships, for arraying of Men for the Marches, and for Defence of the Ifle of *Jerfey*, *appointing fuch* in the Record, as *they conceived* moft proper for the Employment to which they were deftined.

In the 17th, it was declared to the Peers and Commons, that, by their Affents, the King had undertaken the War in *France*, and that a Truce was offered by Mediation of the Pope, *which the Sovereign forbore to accept without their good Allowance.* The Lords therefore confulted apart, and the Com-

Commons returned an Anſwer by Sir *William Truſſel*, that they approved of the Truce and of the Pope's Mediation; and farther, that it was their *Advice and Deſire* that the Quarrel might be compoſed.

The Pope's Undertaking proving fruitleſs, and Delays being of Advantage to the *French*, the King aſſembled the Parliament the Year following, at which Time the Peers and Commons, after many Days Conſultation, *reſolve to end the Conteſt*, either by offering Battle or propoſing Peace, and no more to rely on the Mediation of his Holineſs.

In the 21ſt Year, Chief Juſtice *Thorpe* declared to the Parliament that the *French* War firſt began by their Advice, that the Truce was afterwards accepted by their Aſſent, and that being now expired, it was the King's Pleaſure to have their Council in the farther Proſecution of the War. The Commons being commanded, *Que ils ſe deveroyent trait enſemble & ſe qu'ils enſentercient monſtrer au roy & au gravitur de ſon Conſilio.*

In the 25th, a Parliament was ſummoned to adviſe the King with Relation to the *French* Concerns: And for *more quick Diſpatch*, his Majeſty ordered the Commons to *elect Twenty-four or Thirty* of their Houſe to conſult with the Lords.

In

In the 27th, a Parliament was affembled to confult concerning the Profecution of the *French* War, when honourable Peace could not be obtained; but the Year following a Truce being offered, the King *refufed to ac-cept* the Propofal, *until he had the Confent of the Peers and Commons; which they granted to him by public Inftrument in Parliament before the Pope's Notary.*

In the 36th Year, he called a Parliament to confult whether he fhould declare War againft the King of *Scots,* or conclude Peace with him.

In the 7th Year of *Richard* the 2d, the Commons were commanded to confult *upon View of Articles of Peace with the* FRENCH, whether War or fuch an Accommodation fhould be accepted. They modeftly excufe themfelves as too weak to advife in fuch weighty Affairs. But being charged again as they tendered the Honour and Right of the King, they made this Anfwer; *Quils in-tendent que aucunes fermes & terres que mefme leur Liege auroit oil pur ceft accord in Guien, fi ferront tenu debt Roy Francois par homage & fervice, mais ne perfont uny que leur dit Liege voiroit affenter trope legierement de temer dicens Francois per tiel fervice la Ville de Callis & aultres terres conquifes des Francoife per les-preneve verroit la comen en fe faeft fait, fi au-treme*nt

4

trement lour perroit bien faire, giving their Opinions rather for Peace than War.

In the 13th of *Richard* the 2d, the Truce with *France* being expired, the Parliament was fummoned to advife *upon what Conditions it fhould be renewed*.

In the Year following a Parliament was called, and the King afked Advice of the Lords and Commons concerning the War with *Scotland*, and *would not, without their Counfels, conclude a final Peace* with *France*.

In the 17th Year, the King called a Parliament to confult about the Treaty of Peace with *France*, and the Commons, being charged upon their Faith and Allegiance, advifed that Homage might be made for *Guien*, an Appendage of the *French* Crown, fo as not to include other Parts of the *Englifh* Conqueft.

Henry the 4th confulted with his Parliament on the fame Subjects: Particularly in the tenth Year of his Reign, when the Parliament was commanded to give their Advice about the Truce with *Scotland*, and the Preparations againft the Malice of the *French*.

His Son, in the firft Year of his Reign, advifed with his Parliament how to fuccour his Allies and reftrain his Enemies; and for

E   this

this Purpofe there was a fecret Committee of the Commons appointed to confer with the Lords.

Two Years afterwards Peace being offered by the *French* King, and the King of the *Romans* being arrived to conclude the Bufinefs, *the King refufed to come to any Determination, before he had the Advice and Affent of the Lords and Commons,* which the Chancellor declared to be the End of the Meeting.

In the fourth and fifth Years, no Peace being concluded with *France,* he fummoned the Parliament to confult about a War ; and concluded a Treaty of Amity with *Sigifmund* King of the *Romans,* by *Allowance of the three Eftates*; and the Articles were entered upon the Journal Rolls.

In the eleventh Year, the *Treaty with* France *was perufed and ratified by the Prelates, Nobles, and Commons of the Kingdom.*

His Son, in the fecond Year of his Reign, advifed with the Lords and Commons about preferving the Peace with *France :* And in the third Year, they were called together to *advife upon, and confent to,* a *new Article* in the League with *Scotland.*

The like Inftances may be found in the Reign of *Edward* IV. and others. Even that defpotic Monarch, *Henry* VIII. condefcended

fcended to advife with his Parliament on fuch and other weighty Matters *.

It muft be confeffed, however, that in his Time, but more efpecially in the Reign of Queen *Elizabeth*, the Practice of advifing with Parliament on thefe important Points began to decline, and the Cuftom of referring fuch Confiderations to a minifterial Junto, gradually took place.

We all know in what a lofty Tone her Majefty ufed fometimes to addrefs her Parliament, forbidding them *to meddle with high Concerns of State*. But though, in Words, fhe prohibited them from fuch Confultation, yet, in fact, fhe now and then permitted them to give, nay, folicited, their Advice.

Her Succeffor, *James* I. obftinately tenacious of Prerogative, and more jealous of his own Parliament than of foreign Powers, took all Opportunities of reftraining the Freedom of Debate by his proverbial Check, *Ne futor ultra crepidam.*

Parliaments now began to lofe their Dignity. They were no longer confidered as Channels for Inftruction, but as Mines for

* For Inftances where our Kings confulted with Parliaments on other weighty Matters befides War and Peace, fee the great Antiquary Sir *Robert Cotton.*

Wealth :

Wealth : Minifters did not dive there for Advice, but dig for Ore.

His unhappy Son and Succeffor, *Charles* I. was tempted to purfue the fame unconftitutional Syftem of Policy, and attempted to govern wholly by minifterial Influence.

But the Parliament, weary and afhamed of their own Infignificance, refolved to affert their Importance, and, without being confulted, took the Liberty of remonftrating. The calamitous Effects which thefe Remonftrances produced, are fo well known, that I may fpare myfelf the Trouble and Mortification of repeating the melancholy Detail.

Some time before, and after, the cruel and unparalleled Execution of that unfortunate Prince, Parliaments, if they may be fo called, were one Hour every thing, and the next nothing. A deplorable Succeffion of Anarchy, Oligarchy, Stratocracy, and Tyranny alternately tore the Conftitution and diftracted the Kingdom.

At the *Refloration*, Parliaments once more recovered their antient Form, but did not regain their wonted Influence. An indolent and voluptuous Monarch, bound by Obligations on one Hand, and diverted by Purfuits of Pleafure on the other, refigned all his Concerns to the Direction of a chofen few,

few. In what Manner the Bufinefs of State was conducted during this Reign by a private Junto, we need only confult *Clarendon* and other Writers.

His bigotted Brother and Succeffor, *James* II. juftly provoked the Parliament once again to affert their Authority. To their memorable and glorious Struggle in the Caufe of Freedom, we owe the happy REVOLUTION, which may be confidered as the Æra of *Britifh* Liberty, though, alas! at the fame time the Epoch of Corruption.

At that Time our valuable Rights were confirmed, and the Subject's Paffage to the Throne declared legal. But they were no fooner granted, than fome were fecretly purchafed, and others artfully eluded.

A Fund of Venality was eftablifhed, which made it unneceffary for Minifters to advife with Parliaments, to whom they had the Means of dictating. Our Liberties were mouldering in Fact, while they were ftill frefh upon Record.

You, Sir, have been witnefs to the Arts of Corruption. It is many Years fince your youthful Ardour firft contributed to check its Progrefs and defeat its Defigns.

You have happily furvived to fill a Poft in the Adminiftration, where you have an

Oppor-

Opportunity of enforcing by your Practice, those Principles which you then so nobly urged and supported.

You have made such speedy Advances to this great End, as will do lasting Honour to your Administration. You have banished Corruption infused Vigour into our Councils, established Unanimity in Parliament, and retrieved the Honour of the Kingdom.

Yet all is not done. It remains for you to restore that entire Confidence between the King and his Parliament, which antiently subsisted when that august Assembly was in reality the *Grand Council of the Nation.*

I have been the more particular in producing Instances, where our Kings used formerly, among other Subjects, to consult with their Parliaments with respect to War and Peace, and in shewing how such an amiable Confidence was at length interrupted, left the Method of Negociation which I propose, should be thought innovating and unconstitutional.

It is observable from the Examples I have above cited, that our wisest and greatest Princes have been most forward in advising with their Parliament; and we find that they absolutely refused to conclude *Treaties of Peace,* till the Parliament, *upon a View of the*

6

the Articles, had given their *Advice and Confent*.

It appears, indeed, from the Records, that the Commons, when called upon to advife concerning the Profecution of a War, or to confult whether War or Peace was moft eligible, frequently declined intermedling with fuch weighty Concerns, and witheld their Deliberations, till preffed by their King's Command.

The Reafon of this Modefty and Referve on thefe Occafions, is obvious to every one of common Sagacity. We do not find however, that when called upon merely to deliberate upon the fole Subject of Peace, that they ever made any fuch modeft Hefitations. The Reafon no longer fubfifted.

No Objection feems now to offer againft reviving this antient and conftitutional Cuftom of advifing with Parliament. Why fhould lefs Diftinction and Confidence be paid to that auguft Affembly now than formerly? Rather why fhould they not be honoured with higher Marks of Favour and Truft?

Since the Revolution, the Column of public Freedom ftands on a broader Bafis: And confequently inftead of requiring Diminution, the Superftructure will admit of Enlargement.

Par-

Parliaments, neverthelefs, have too long ceafed to be what they were at their original Inftitution, and what they always ought to be, *the Grand Council of the Nation.* The Members of which it is compofed, have been too long confidered rather as the Bankers, than the Counfellors of the Kingdom : And Minifters have drawn upon *them* for *Money,* while they have taken *Counfel* of their own Pride and Intereft.

We can now, indeed, happily boaft of a Minifter, who acts upon more juft and enlarged Principles. A fair Opportunity now prefents itfelf of reftoring Parliaments to their antient, true, and refpectable Condition.

Shall the People who have fo chearfully and vigoroufly exerted themfelves in the Profecution of the War, be deemed not worthy of being confulted at the Conclufion of a Peace ?

Shall they who have purchafed fo many glorious Acquifitions by their Blood and Treafure, have the Mortification to find them difpofed of by a Treaty concluded in private ? Shall the Articles be kept from their Infpection, till the Ratification of them has made it too late for them to offer Objections and propofe Amendments? Shall they who are chief *Parties* to the Negociation, not be *Privies* to it ?

Such

Such a Proceeding might, at any time, be confidered as unjuft, unnatural, and repugnant to the Idea of that Confidence, which ought ever to fubfift between a King and a free People.

But at fuch a Crifis as this, it would appear uncommonly hard and unkind. The prefent Parliament have fhewn a moft laudable Zeal and Attachment to his Majefty's Perfon and Government; they have preferved an Unanimity which has done themfelves no lefs Honour than their Country Service, and they have readily granted Supplies which even exceed Credibility. For thefe diftinguifhed Proofs of Loyalty, Wifdom, and Generofity, they undoubtedly merit a more than common Degree of Confidence.

His Majefty, who has been gracioufly pleafed, in his Speech from the Throne, to exprefs his Satisfaction in the happy Union which has fubfifted among them, has now an Opportunity of rewarding their Merit, by calling Them to fhare in thofe councils to which their Forefathers were admitted: A Confidence to which they have the ftrongeft conftitutional Claim, fince, without their Advice, his Royal Predeceffors refufed to conclude Treaties of Peace, or any other important Negociations.

F

No

No Time can be more opportune for re-eftablifhing this defireable Intercourfe and Confidence between the King and his Parliament. They are in the moft proper Difpofition to confult. No Party Animofities will thwart their Debates, no difaffected Oppofition will perplex their Confultations.

The *Matter* of Debate likewife favours their Interpofition. The approaching Treaty requires more Deliberation than Difpatch. But fhould Expedition be requifite, we might purfue the Example of our Anceftors in fuch Cafes, and depute a felect Number of the Commons, Forty, for Inftance, (the Number which conftitutes a Houfe) to confult with the Lords on the important Negociation which lies in Profpect.

But happily we can treat our Enemies as the Whig Miniftry treated the Negotiators of the Peace of Utrecht *. We can make them ftand at the Out-fide of the Clofet, while we at our Leifure determine their Fate within: And our Deliberations need not be fecret.

As no Obftacle, therefore, in my humble Apprehenfion, oppofes this Mode of Nego-

* Had that Treaty, which, in fome meafure, laid the Foundation of the prefent War, been debated in Parliament, the Terms, in all probability, would not have been fo equivocal, inglorious, and unprofitable.

ciation, why fhould not the approaching
Treaty be conducted agreeably to the old and
conftitutional Method?

The Glory, Sir, of reviving this Practice,
which Tyranny firft fufpended, and Corruption afterwards effaced, is referved for you.
In a Government conftituted like ours, much,
almoft every thing, depends on the Skill and
Patriot Efforts of a Minifter.

As Treaties abftracted from Neceffity do
not bind States without fome Degree of moral Equity to enforce their Obfervance, fo
municipal Laws have no Weight in particular Conftitutions, unlefs public-fpirited Principles in the executive and minifterial Branch,
co-operate with the legiflative Authority.

Should a Minifter prove void of national
Zeal and Integrity, the *Bill of Rights* would
be as obfolete as the greateft part of *Magna
Charta.* Paper and Parchment may be good
Vouchers, but they are weak Guardians, of
our Liberties. If we have no better Security,
we may have Reafon to exclaim with the Poet,
Quid Leges fine Moribus vanæ proficiunt?

I own, Sir, that I am anxious to reftore
the Dignity and Authority of Parliament;
and

and I think the approaching Negociation a favourable Occasion for reviving it.

You, who have ingenuously displayed your Plan of Operations with such engaging Frank-ness and Integrity, during the Course of the War, can have no Desire of concluding a Peace in Privacy.

You have throughout your whole Admi-niftration conducted yourself with an Open-nefs and Sincerity, which has attached all difinterested Men to your Service. You have wisely kept no Secrets, but where the Dif-covery of your Designs might put the Enemy on their Guard, and thereby fruftrate the Execution of your Schemes.

I am thoroughly satisfied therefore of your Inclinations, to co-operate in any Proposal for re-eftablifhing the Reputation and Power of Parliament on its original Foundation.

But I need not speak of *my* Persuasions, your Country is convinced of your Patriot Intentions. Your Fellow-Citizens gratefully unite in extolling your Probity, and admiring your Capacity.

Persuaded, therefore, of your sincere In-clinations to promote the End which I have

in

in View, fhould you difapprove of the Propofal, I fhall think myfelf unhappy in having recommended indifcreet Means.

Yet pardon me, Sir, if at prefent I judge
the Means to be as conducive to your, and
the general Intereft, as the End, I am convinced, is to your Inclinations. You feem to
have lefs Profpect of acquiring Reputation by
a Treaty privately managed, than by one open-
ly conducted. In the firft Cafe, Envy and Malice will be forward to attribute its Merit to
unknown Affiftance, and its Imperfections to
yourfelf : In the latter, you would publickly
fhare the Glory, and your Country would reap
Honour and Advantage, by a Mode of Negociation calculated to revive the Influence of
Parliaments.

As all Circumftances, therefore, feem to
favour, as every Confideration feems to direct,
the Revival of this antient and conftitutional
Method of proceeding, we may hope to fee
the Articles of the enfuing Treaty laid before
Parliament, and debated by that auguft Affembly, before they are ratified by Plenipotentiaries.

This will be no Invafion of the Prerogative. The Power of denouncing War, and

3   con-

concluding Peace, will ftill remain with the Sovereign : And the Confultation in Parliament, being in confequence of the King's Permiffion and Defire, will be a Matter of *Grace*, not of *Right*.

The good Effect of this happyConfidence, will be more extenfive than is readily to be conceived. Europe, which has beheld the Power of our Arms with Amazement, will view this Inftance of the Freedom and Harmony of our Government with Admiration ; and will be deterred from attempting to difturb a Kingdom fo firmly united.

Our gracious Sovereign's Inclinations to contribute every thing in his Power to promote the Happinefs, and fecure the Freedom of his People, are well known. It depends upon you, Sir, if you approve of the Propofal, to point out the projected Means, which, among others, lead to this defirable End.

By your Endeavours, we hope to fee the Work of Reformation compleated. The reftoring the Dignity of Parliament, the Independance of the Conftitution, the Eftablifhment of Oeconomy, and the Revival of Moral Virtue, are Bleffings expected at your Hands.

Hands. The Public Hopes reft upon you. *Si Tu deferis, actum eft !*

Before I conclude, permit me to take Notice of the Letter-writer's judicious and fpirited Reprefentation, of the Dangers to which our Conftitution is expofed at *Home.*—Dangers which he defcribes with fuch real Concern, and paints in fuch ftrong Colours, as at once do Honour to the Author's Zeal and Abilities.

His Reflections, in thefe refpects, feem to merit moft ferious Confideration. His Apprehenfions in particular of the Mifchiefs which may arife from too numerous a *Standing Army* in time of Peace, appear to be too juftly founded.

" I lament," fays this animated Writer, " to fee the Sentiments of the Nation fo amazingly reconciled to the Profpect of having a far more numerous Body of regular Troops kept up, after the Peace, than any true Lover of his Country, in former Times, thought could be allowed, without endangering the Conftitution."

Undoubtedly the prefent extravagant Fondnefs for military Eftablifhments of every Kind, muft alarm all true Lovers of their Country, who

who are capable of extending their Thoughts
to Confequences.

You may remember, Sir, when our Pa-
triots, about the Years 1737 and 1738, were
fo jealous of military Power, that they would
fcarce endure the Beat of a Drum within
hearing of the Metropolis. Now they fee,
without Concern, our Palaces converted into
Barracks; and are become fo fond of Soldiers
that they would even quarter them in their
dwelling Houfes.

In all free States, where the Paffions have
their full Scope, the Public are generally extravagant in their Attachments, or violent in
their Averfions.

All fuch Exceffes, however, are every way
to be dreaded: And I wifh, that, when the
Conclufion of a Peace has made our military
Gentlemen no longer of immediate Service,
an ungrateful Averfion may not take Place of
this immoderate Fondnefs.

In the View of fober Confideration, we
ought, in time of Peace, to look upon Soldiers as Men who, though immediately bur-
thenfome and unferviceable, have been, and
may hereafter be, ufeful: And in time of
War, as Men who, though of prefent Uti-
lity,

lity, have been, and may hereafter be, troublesome and dangerous.

To consider them in this Light, will teach us Gratitude towards them for their past Services, and learn us Caution to guard against the Dangers with which their Power may threaten us hereafter.

It will require all your Skill and Attention, Sir, how to dispose of the redundant military Force, on the Conclusion of a Peace. Something may be thought due to a Number of brave Men, who have so gloriously ventured their Lives in the Service of their Country: Some Provision should be thought of, that they may not be under a Necessity of prowling about, to the Terror, and perhaps to the Detriment, of their Fellow-Citizens.

Something likewife is due to the Safety of the Nation. At all Events, the present military Propensity, against which the Letter-writer so justly inveighs, ought to be checked.

It is at the Time when over zealous Fools ridicule Caution, and call it Mistrust, that Mischiefs imperceptibly steal upon the Constitution.

G   Our

Our beft and moft popular Princes and Minifters have generally laid the Foundation of thofe Misfortunes, which were fatally experienced at fucceeding Periods. Their Succeffors, being invefted with the fame Power without the fame good Inclinations, changed that Confidence into a Curfe, which in the Hands of their Predeceffors was a Blefling to the Nation. It is in this Refpect alone, that we have any thing to fear from his Majefty, or his Minifters.

I fpeak thus freely, without any Apprehenfion of giving Offence. I fpeak of a King who does not wifh to extend the Prerogative : I fpeak to a Miuifter, who covets no Power inconfiftent with the Conftitution.

With fuch Difpofitions therefore in his Majefty and his Servants, what fhould prevent Parliaments from being reftored to their former Influence and Importance ? We may be affured that no fubordinate Authority will be truly refpectable, while that is held in light Efteem.

Should Parliaments ever be again, what we know they have been, Machines moved

2   by

by fecret minifterial Springs; fhould they affemble tutored before-hand, and repeat the Leffon of Servility, or with mute Submiffion ftoop to be counted, on a Divifion, among the Herd of Venality; fhould they, who are fummoned together to decide on the important Points of religious, moral and political Duties, know no other God than Mammon, no other Virtue than Pliability, no other Policy than Self-Intereft; fhould they be the Creatures of thofe over whom they fhould fuperintend, and be worfe than Cyphers in the Service of their Conftituents; fhould they wantonly, indolently, or corruptly vote away the Treafure of the Kingdom, without making any Inquiry into the Application; fhould they be confidered as the Purfebearers of their Conftituents, rather than as the grand Counfellors of the State—How would their Dignity be impaired? How would the Honour and Welfare of the Nation be endangered?

Where public Virtue is wanting, all national Succefs is only tranfitory. It is like a rich Legacy to a Spendthrift; it ferves to pamper Luxury, and accelerate his Ruin. Nothing but religious and moral Principles can enable us to fecure the Advantages

we

we have acquired, and enfure our Prof-
perity.

Thefe Principles cannot be expected to
actuate the People, where they do not appear to influence the Parliament. If *they* do
not preferve their Virtue and affert their Dignity, the People will copy their Manners,
and become corrupt and abject.

The late Revival of public Spirit, is a re-
cent Proof of the powerful Effects of parliamentary Influence. The Unanimity and patriot Zeal which that auguft Body has fhewn
through the Courfe of the War, has diffufed
itfelf over Men of all Ranks and Denomi-
nations.

The Love of our Country, thank Heaven,
is no longer an Object of Ridicule, but confidered as a ferious Duty: And Inftances of
public Generofity, Benevolence and Humanity daily multiply.

It is no Flattery, Sir, to pronounce you
the chief Inftrument of this happy Change.
Would you have the Effects of your Adminiftration furvive your Power; would you
complete the glorious Work of Reformation; would you be a Favourite of the wife
and

and good; would you have your Name live to future Ages, and be honoured in the Grave;—Begin by fupporting the Dignity, and reviving the true and original Ufe of Parliaments.

Should they lofe their Importance, they will never long maintain their Independance. When they know that they are but Machines, they will naturally act mechanically. Such as they are, fuch will be their Conftituents : For the far greater Part of Mankind act by Imitation. May our Reprefentatives therefore ever be fenfible of their Dignity! And may Virtue become the Fafhion !

You, Sir, have contributed much to this defirable End. Yet much remains to be done. I am fenfible of the Obftructions which the Principles of fome, and the Inte-reft of others, will raife to check your Progrefs towards farther Reformation. I am not fo little converfant with the World, as not to know that there are many fecret Murmurers againft you, who only wait for the flighteft Opportunity of being loud in Oppofition.

But this is not all. The long Neglect and Ridicule of every ferious Duty, and the avowed Maxim of governing by Corruption,

has

has debafed fome of the nobleft Minds, and fettled Habits of Depravity, which only Time and Perfeverance can conquer. *Confummata eft infelicitas, ubi, quæ fuerunt vitia, mores funt.*

Yet every thing is to be expected from your Prudence, Spirit, and Virtue. But I do not mean to write your Panegyrick. Let your future Conduct be your Elogium. That will fpeak a Language which cannot lie: But the Pen of Adulation, Sir, is as current in the Service of a *Sejanus* as of a *Sully.*

If what I have had the Honour to propofe, fhould be deemed in the leaft Degree conducive to the great End of *improving* the Confidence between the King and his Parliament, and of giving additional Weight to that auguft Body, I fhall think myfelf happy in having fuggefted the Thought.

It becomes me, however, Sir, to apologize to you, and to the Public, for thefe rude and hafty Sketches. But had I Power to command the Graces of Writing, my Eagernefs to communicate a Propofal, which to me appeared fo expedient, would have fruftrated my Endeavours towards Improvement and Elegance.

I am

I am more anxious of meriting the Diftinction of a zealous Citizen, than ambitious
of gaining Applaufe as a good Writer.

I have the Honour to be,

With real Refpect,

Sir,

Your moft obedient,

And moft humble Servant,

The AUTHOR.

F I N I S.

ERRATUM.

Page 15, Line 2, for *Pagonum*, read *Pagorum*.

www.ingramcontent.com/pod-product-compliance
Lightning Source LLC
Chambersburg PA
CBHW031816090426
42739CB00008B/1294